E. B. White

The Library of Author Biographies™

E. B. WHITE

Deb Aronson

The Rosen Publishing Group, Inc., New York

Published in 2005 by The Rosen Publishing Group, Inc.
29 East 21st Street, New York, NY 10010

Copyright © 2005 by The Rosen Publishing Group, Inc.

First Edition

Library of Congress Cataloging-in-Publication Data

Aronson, Deb.
E. B. White / by Deb Aronson.— 1st ed.
  p. cm. — (The library of author biographies)
Includes bibliographical references (p.) and index.
ISBN 1-4042-0326-5 (lib. bdg.)
1. White, E. B. (Elwyn Brooks), 1899– 2. Authors, American—20th century—Biography. 3. Children's stories—Authorship.
I. Title. II. Series.
PS3545.H5187Z525 2004
818'.5209—dc22

2004013384

Manufactured in the United States of America

Excerpt from *E. B. White* by Scott Elledge. Copyright © 1985 & 1984 by Scott Elledge. Used by permission of W. W. Norton & Company, Inc.
Excerpt from *E. B. White* by Edward C. Sampson, Twayne Publishers, copyright © 1974, Twayne Publishers. Reprinted by permission of the Gale Group.
Excerpt from the *Horn Book Magazine*, September/October 1988. Reprinted by permission of the Horn Book, Inc., Boston, MA, www.hbook.com.
Text reprinted by permission; copyright © 1999 John Updike.
Originally published in the *New Yorker*. All rights reserved.
For more *New Yorker* articles, please visit www.newyorker.com.
Excerpt from *Children's Books and Their Creators*, edited by Anita Silvey. Copyright © 1995 by Houghton Mifflin Company. Reprinted by permission of Houghton Mifflin Company. All rights reserved.
Excerpt from *Something About the Author* Vol. 29, by Gale Group, copyright © 1982, Gale Group. Reprinted by permission of the Gale Group.
Text © 1973 by the University of Chicago. All rights reserved.
Cornell University Library, as owners of the physical object only, grants Rosen Publishing Group, Inc., permission to quote from the E. B. White Collection, 1899–1985, Number 7564, courtesy of the Division of Rare and Manuscript Collections, Cornell University Library. Permission granted by the E.B. White Estate.
Text from *Trumpet of the Swan*. Copyright © 1970 by E. B. White. Used with the permission of HarperCollins Children's Books.
Text from *Charlotte's Web*. Copyright © 1952 by E. B. White. © renewed 1980 by E. B. White. Used with the permission of HarperCollins Children's Books.

Table of Contents

Introduction:
"I Love the World"

In his almost eighty-year writing career, E. B. White wrote only three children's books—*Stuart Little* (1945), *Charlotte's Web* (1952), and *The Trumpet of the Swan* (1970)—but each one is among the best-loved children's books ever written. White loved life. As he once wrote in a letter to a fan, "All I hope to say in books . . . is that I love the world. You can find that in there [in my writing], if you dig around."[1] This world that White spoke of lovingly revolved around animals.

As a child, he had numerous pets, from dogs to pigeons. As an adult, he lived on a farm, which was filled with animals such as sheep, geese, and pigs. And he always had at least one dog. It is no coincidence that all three of White's children's books have animals as the main characters. *Stuart Little* is about a small, mouse-sized boy with mouse-sized features and the adventures he has. *Charlotte's Web* is about a runty pig named Wilbur who makes friends with a clever spider who then saves Wilbur's life. And *The Trumpet of the Swan* is about the adventures of Louis, a trumpeter swan who was born unable to make any sounds, including the signature trumpeting sound of his species.

In fact, all of his life, White preferred animals to people and nature to polite society. But his books are not just about animals and nature. White's animal characters participate in the human world. For example, despite his long tail and pointy ears, Stuart Little is born to a human family. And Wilbur, who lives on a farm, is also part of a community of humans. His first savior is a little girl named Fern. In *The Trumpet of the Swan*, Louis the swan chooses to interact with people in order to help him solve various problems. Hence, even though White wrote about animals and their adventures, his stories are also about important human qualities and feelings. As Edward C. Sampson wrote in his book *E. B. White*

(1974), "There is much to be learned from White's stories, to be sure, but it is not geography, or science, or even the habit of mice and pigs. What the child does learn . . . is a great deal about loyalty, honesty, love, sadness, and happiness."[2]

Throughout his career, White would earn many awards for his writing. In 1963, he received the Presidential Medal of Freedom from President John F. Kennedy. In 1970, he received the Laura Ingalls Wilder Award. And in 1978, he was awarded a special Pulitzer Prize citation for lifetime literary achievement. However, E. B. White did not write in order to receive awards, to earn a lot of money, or even to be famous. As he once said, "Like any good writer, I write to amuse myself, not some imaginary audience."[3]

Although White is perhaps best known for his children's books, he wrote more for adults. His essays, poems, and columns discussing current events regularly appeared in two well-known magazines for adults, the *New Yorker* and *Harper's*. However, White's children's books were the longest single pieces he ever wrote. He enjoyed writing for young people because he felt they had better imaginations. They didn't have trouble accepting situations such as a mouse-like boy being in a human family or a spider that befriends a pig.

Meanwhile, critics and fellow writers praised White's writing style for its precise language and gentle humor. White doesn't use very many big words or words borrowed from other languages. Instead, he sounds like your next-door neighbor, only funnier. When you read something by White, it feels like a friend is just telling you a story. "He had a gift of inspiring affection in the reader,"[4] a writer in the *New Yorker* magazine wrote after White died.

It is not uncommon for writers to struggle at their craft, and in White's case, writing was always painfully difficult. Even though his style was relaxed and simple, it took a lot of work to make the words flow so effortlessly. In fact, White spent as much time avoiding his typewriter as he did writing with it. Once, White compared writing to a sneeze, suggesting that it was something he couldn't control or resist. He couldn't bear to write, but he also couldn't bear not to.

Readers around the world are lucky that White didn't give up and stop writing. His books have remained popular among both young people and adults for more than fifty years. This puts White's work in the category of enduring classic stories that include other such masterpieces as Kenneth Grahame's *Wind in the Willows* (1908), Dick King-Smith's *Babe the Gallant Pig* (1984), and Hugh Lofting's *Dr. Dolittle* (1920).

1 Growing Up

Elwyn Brooks (E. B.) White was born on July 11, 1899, in Mt. Vernon, New York. Elwyn was the youngest of six children (a seventh, Janet, died in infancy). His siblings were all much older than he was. When Elwyn was born, Lillian, who was the next youngest, was five, and Marion, the oldest, was eighteen. By the time Elwyn was twelve, all his siblings had left home. His two oldest sisters, Marion and Clara, were married, his two brothers, Albert and Stanley, had finished college and were working, and his youngest sister, Lillian, was in college.

When Elwyn was born, his parents were fairly old. His father, Samuel Tilly White, was forty-five, and his mother, Jessie Hart, was forty-one.

Elwyn's mother chose her son's unusual name because she had met a boy named Elwyn whom she liked very much. He was the son of a friend, and she had always admired his name, which is Welsh for "pale brow." During his childhood, Elwyn's name was shortened to "En" by his family and friends. This was mostly because he detested the name Elwyn.

Happy and Safe

Elwyn's childhood was happy and safe. He had a close and loving family. Elwyn's father, Samuel, worked his whole life at the Horace Waters Piano Company. He had started there at age thirteen as an errand boy. A few years before Elwyn was born, Samuel moved the family from Brooklyn to a large house he had built in Mt. Vernon.

Elwyn's parents were proud of their spacious home. Elwyn especially liked the octagonal tower room. Every day, Samuel White took a thirty-minute train ride from Mt. Vernon to Grand Central Station in New York City to go to work. He worked in Manhattan, one of five boroughs, or districts, that make up New York City. The other boroughs are the Bronx, Brooklyn, Staten Island, and Queens.

By the time Elwyn was born, his father was the vice president of the Waters company. Samuel was settled enough in his career to be able to devote more time to his family, and Elwyn benefited greatly from his father's affection and attention. Although Elwyn's father had to leave school when he was thirteen, he loved learning and was fascinated by the English language. One way Samuel shared this interest with his children was to send them over to the household copy of *Webster's Unabridged Dictionary* when they heard or read an unfamiliar word. The dictionary was so big, the only place for it was on a cast-iron stand in one of Elwyn's brother's bedrooms.

Love of Animals

Even though Elwyn's childhood was happy and safe, he still was timid and anxious. It was simply the kind of personality he was born with. As Elwyn later wrote in an essay:

> As a child, I was frightened but not unhappy. I lacked for nothing except confidence. I suffered nothing except the routine terrors of childhood: fear of the dark, fear of the future,

fear of the return to school after a summer on a lake in Maine, fear of making an appearance on a platform, fear of the lavatory [bathroom] in the school basement where the slate urinals cascaded, fear that I was unknowing about things I should know about.[1]

Elwyn wasn't an outgoing child who felt the need for the company of many people. Nevertheless, he played with the neighborhood children and had some childhood friends. When he was growing up, Elwyn loved being outdoors. He loved to ice skate, go for bike rides, and climb trees. His very first dog was a collie named Mac. Elwyn loved Mac, but the dog was not allowed in the house. Because of this, Elwyn built an elaborate sheepskin-lined doghouse for Mac in the barn. Elwyn also collected and raised pigeons, canaries, lizards, and turtles.

One of the most exciting moments of his life was the first time Elwyn saw chicks hatching. He had to stand on his tiptoes to see the fifty eggs warming on a table under the incubator in the family stable. He would never forget the thrill of seeing the first chicks coming out. In fact, for the rest of his life as a writer, Elwyn would use the image of an egg to represent the miracle of life. He thought it was amazing that a life could come from something as cold and hard as an egg.

Years later, when he wrote *The Trumpet of the Swan*, Elwyn's feelings about an egg are summed up by the character of Sam Beaver. Sam writes in his journal:

> I don't know of anything in the entire world more wonderful to look at than a nest with eggs in it. An egg, because it contains life, is the most perfect thing there is. It is beautiful and mysterious. An egg is a far finer thing than a tennis ball or a cake of soap. A tennis ball will always be just a tennis ball. A cake of soap will always be just a cake of soap . . . But an egg will someday be a living creature . . .[2]

Fear of Speaking

Although he did well in school, Elwyn found it very boring. It was hard for him to sit still when he preferred being outside or tending to his pets. It was in elementary school that he developed his lifelong fear of and anxiety about public speaking. Every year, students had to recite a poem in front of the whole school. To determine in what order students would speak, the teachers called on them by going through their names in alphabetical order according to their last names. Often, a whole year would pass without Elwyn's name being called.

A shy and self-conscious boy when he was in public, Elwyn lived in dread of being called on. If he made it safely through the year without being picked, the following year, the teachers started again at the top of the list with the letter A. Elwyn was called on only once, when he was in fifth grade. He tried to recite a poem by Henry Wadsworth Longfellow, but he garbled the words and the whole thing was an embarrassing disaster for him.

Regardless of his mistakes, he still might have been able to continue, but he heard giggling in the audience. That made him forget the entire poem. He was devastated and swore he would never again speak in public. And he never did. Much later, when he was an established writer, he often refused awards and other honors, especially if they required giving a speech. He sometimes wrote speeches that others read for him, but never once did he actually give one himself.

Early Success

Although he hated speaking in front of others, at an early age, Elwyn knew that he loved to write. In 1947, when Elwyn was forty-eight, he wrote to his brother Stanley and stated, "I took to writing early, to assuage [relieve] my uneasiness and collect my thoughts . . . I remember, really quite distinctly, looking at a sheet of paper square in the eyes when I was seven or eight years old and thinking 'This is where I belong, this is it.'"[3] About this time, Elwyn began to write in a journal, which he would keep faithfully for the next fifteen to twenty years.

Aside from keeping a journal, Elwyn also began writing stories. In 1909, at the age of ten, he won his first writing prize for a poem about a mouse. The contest was sponsored by *Woman's Home Companion*, a popular women's magazine at the time. Elwyn enjoyed winning and having his name mentioned in the magazine, even though when listing his prize, the magazine editors misspelled his name as "Elwin."

Elwyn also submitted many pieces to *St. Nicholas Magazine*, a high-quality, well-respected national magazine for children that was published between 1873 and 1939. *St. Nicholas* printed fiction by some of the best-known children's writers of the day, including Frances Hodgson Burnett, author of *The Secret Garden* (1909); Robert Louis Stevenson, author of *Treasure Island* (1883); Mark Twain, author of *The Adventures of Tom Sawyer* (1876) and *The Adventures of Huckleberry Finn*

(1884); and Louisa May Alcott, author of *Little Women* (1868).

St. Nicholas Magazine had a section in which young writers could submit their poetry, prose, photographs, and drawings. This section was known as the St. Nicholas League. Membership in the league was free, and every month, children from all over the United States and England joined and submitted work. Competition was fierce. Many of Elwyn's friends also submitted work.

When he was eleven, Elwyn received a silver badge from *St. Nicholas Magazine* for a short story he wrote, titled "A Winter Walk." When he was fourteen, he won the coveted gold badge. His winning story, titled "A True Dog Story," was about a boy's adventures with his dog. The dog in the story was based on the family's Irish setter.

This was the beginning of Elwyn's long career of writing about what he loved most of all: animals and the people who befriend them. In fact, his early success at *St. Nicholas* gave him the encouragement to continue writing.

Belgrade Lakes

For Elwyn, the best part of growing up was the time he spent with his family at Belgrade Lakes in central Maine. Elwyn's family went to Maine, in part, because Elwyn suffered from terrible hay fever. The family doctor thought going somewhere farther north might ease some of his symptoms.

Hence, every summer, beginning in 1905, Elwyn's parents would pack up the family, including Beppo (their Irish setter), and travel by the Bar Harbor Express train to Belgrade. It was a twelve-hour train ride. A farm wagon would then carry the entire family the last ten miles (sixteen kilometers) to a cabin by the shore. At Belgrade Lakes, Elwyn learned to sail. Sailing would ultimately become a life-long passion for him. He also canoed on the lake with his brother Stanley.

Stanley, who was a gentle and patient teacher, taught his little brother about the flora and fauna of the lake and shore. Stanley and Elwyn always had a close relationship. When they were young, Stanley taught Elwyn many other things, too. For example, when Elwyn was about five years old, Stanley taught him how to read by having him sound out words in the *New York Times* newspaper. Because of this, Elwyn could read perfectly by the time he entered first grade.

Love of Nature

In Maine, Elwyn's favorite pastime was to sit outside for hours, simply watching what was going on. Being outside by the lake or in the woods were places he felt most at peace when he was younger. He compared this sensation to how many people feel when they sit in church. Sam Beaver, the main human character in *The Trumpet of the Swan*, shares this love of peacefully sitting and observing nature. Sam Beaver is happiest when he is sitting quietly, watching the swans on the small pond that is their home. When White describes this part of Sam's character in *The Trumpet of the Swan*, he is remembering himself as a boy and the things he loved to do.

2 College and Beyond

U nlike many teens just finishing high school, White already had a good idea of what interested him. He knew he liked to write, he loved nature and raising domestic animals, and he loved sailing. White would be passionate about these things for the rest of his life. After high school, White went to Cornell University in Ithaca, New York, just as his two brothers, Albert and Stanley, had done. White's youngest sister, Lillian, went to Vassar College in Poughkeepsie, New York. His two oldest sisters married and did not attend college.

In college, White had several experiences that would shape the rest of his life. Many of those experiences took place outside of class, but most had to do with writing. At Cornell, White joined the school newspaper, which was called the *Daily Sun*. In his junior year, he became editor in chief, the top position at a newspaper. In 1920, when White was editor in chief, the *Daily Sun* was one of only two daily college newspapers published in the United States. It was also the only morning paper in the town of Ithaca. Because of this, everyone in town read it.

White took his work very seriously—in fact, more seriously than his class assignments. Although he loved being in college, he wasn't an outstanding student. His grades ranged from As to Ds even in his favorite subjects, such as English.

Elements of a Writer

White also joined the Manuscript Club, which was organized and sponsored by a man named Martin Sampson. Sampson was an English professor at Cornell. At Manuscript Club gatherings, professors and students critiqued one another's essays and poems. In this club, White met William Strunk Jr., a professor of English whose influence on him was enormous. Strunk was an advocate of simple, clear writing. One of Strunk's favorite bits of advice was, "Omit [remove] needless words." Years later, White joked in an essay that Strunk's teaching style was so concise that he often ran out of things to say before the class time was over. As a result, he would often repeat himself, "Omit needless words. Omit needless words. Omit needless words."[1]

Professor Strunk's book *The Elements of Style* (1920) was used in every Cornell English class. It was privately printed just for Strunk's classes. In 1957, White wrote an affectionate memoir of his teacher, which appeared in the *New Yorker*. Shortly after that, he agreed to write an introduction and revise Strunk's original text. This revision, first published in 1959, became known as *Strunk and White*. Used by almost every college student taking English, this reference work has sold 100,000 copies annually since 1959.

The Influence of Professors

White got to know other professors who also had a great impact on him. One was Bristow Adams, a journalism professor. On Monday evenings, a group of journalism students would gather at Adams's house in Ithaca to talk about everything from journalism ethics to international events. It was these evenings, more than most classes he took, that helped White learn how to think critically and shape his own opinions. White formed a lifelong friendship with Adams and Adams's wife, Louella. Many years later, he said he felt more at home with them than he did even with his own parents.

A Special Teacher

One class in particular that had a great influence on White was a history of the Middle Ages course taught by a professor named George Lincoln Burr. Burr talked about how people in the Middle Ages suffered from lack of basic freedoms and education. It was during this course that White began to understand and appreciate the importance of freedom, knowledge, and truth. As he would later say:

> My chance encounter with George Lincoln Burr was the greatest single thing that ever happened in my life, for he introduced me to a part of myself that I hadn't discovered. I saw, with blinding clarity, how vital it is for man to live in a free society. The experience enabled [allowed] me to grow up almost overnight; it gave my thoughts and

ambitions a focus. It caused me indirectly to pursue the kind of work which eventually enabled me to earn my living.[2]

And, indeed, throughout his career, White wrote often of the importance of having freedom, fighting for it when necessary, and the responsibilities that come with having freedom.

Cornell Days

White loved the countryside surrounding Cornell. The college is in the middle of the state of New York. The campus is surrounded by hills. There are many trails and places to walk and hike. On his walks, White was usually accompanied by his mongrel dog, Mutt.

Another good thing that happened while White was at Cornell was that he picked up a nickname he would use the rest of his life. Although he usually signed his work "E. B. White" from college on, his friends called him Andy. Why Andy? Because the first president of Cornell was named Andy White, and a tradition had developed that any Cornell student whose last name was White would be called Andy. In White's case, the name stuck for the rest of his life.

After his junior, or third, year of college, White worked at a boys' camp in Dorset, Ontario, which was called Camp Otter. The camp was owned by the physical education instructor at Cornell, and many students worked there. The campers and counselors took numerous canoe trips, built campfires, sang songs, and roasted marshmallows. White loved the camp so much that he worked there again the summer after he graduated from college.

Footloose

Even after White finished college and the summer at Camp Otter was over, he wasn't in a big rush to find a regular, full-time job. The first five or six years after White finished college were filled with adventure but not much steady work. White was not exactly sure what he wanted to do, except he thought it should have something to do with journalism because he knew he wanted to write.

The problem was that even though he really liked to write, he was definitely not interested in full-time office work. He liked his freedom and flexibility too much. In fact, as young as age thirteen, White had written in his journal that he didn't want to have to get up every morning and rush to an office like his father did. All his life, White would try very hard not to have a job where he was expected to report at a certain time every morning and stop working at a specific time every evening.

Nonetheless, White did work at several jobs, starting in the fall of 1921. However, he didn't stick with any of them. Over the span of nine months, he tried out four writing jobs. He found the work either too stressful or too boring, and sometimes both. Accordingly, in February 1922, when White's friend Harold Cushman flunked out of Cornell, the two of them decided to take off on a cross-country driving trip. White quit his job—again—and they left the East Coast in March. White did all the driving (they used his Model T, nicknamed Hotspur) since Cushman didn't know how to drive. Hotspur is a nickname for Harry Percy, a historical figure who was immortalized in *Henry IV, Part I*, a play by William Shakespeare. Hotspur refers to Percy's fiery and uncontrollable temper.

Adventure on the Open Road

White and Cushman didn't have much of a plan for their trip. They each packed a typewriter with the idea that, in order to make money along the way, they could write and sell articles to newspapers and magazines. In 1922, there was no national highway system of paved roads and well-marked signs. These wouldn't come into being for another thirty years. Because of this, their adventure was very different from what it would be like today. The roads were usually two dirt ruts that wound up and down hills. Occasionally, the lane would wander into a town. They used a popular touring book called the *Blue Book* as their guide.

With roads in such poor condition, tires didn't last long. And new tires cost money—money the two young men did not have. Gas and food were also a concern. As they traveled, White and Cushman took odd jobs in order to pay for the trip. In one town, they sandpapered a dance floor. In other places, they did everything from washing dishes, running a concession stand during a carnival, selling roach powder door to door, and working as hay hands. White did sell a couple of poems and a story, but eventually, he needed to sell his typewriter for grocery money. Finally, in Alberta, White walked 32 miles (51 km) to the nearest town, carrying Cushman's typewriter. He traded the typewriter for a tire.

Seattle Times

Soon after they got to Seattle, Washington, White was hired as a journalist at the *Seattle Times* and Cushman returned home. White found it very hard to write articles quickly, and he sometimes missed the deadlines. As he later said when talking about his earlier life:

> I was a flop [failure] as a daily reporter. Every piece had to be a masterpiece—and before you knew it, Tuesday was Wednesday.[3]

Soon, however, White's boss had the idea of White writing feature stories instead of news. Feature stories, which are about interesting people or events, don't have to be written the day the events happen, like news pieces do. White also started writing a column of paragraphs. Sometimes the paragraphs were connected thoughts and sometimes they were not. However, they always commented on things going on in the city. This was a style used by many newspapers at the time. At the *New Yorker*, a magazine White would write for in the late 1920s, that same style was used in the "Notes and Comments" section of the magazine.

Unfortunately, however, only eleven months after he was hired, White lost his job. Although his editor assured him that it had nothing to do with his writing, White was not convinced. He felt terrible about the loss, but in a way he also felt lighthearted. Ultimately, White was not a man who yearned for the security of a job.

More Adventure

After several weeks of hanging around jobless in Seattle, White went down to the docks to see about a job on the steamer *Buford*. When it became clear that there was no work available, he booked a passage to Skagway, Alaska, for $40. He was hoping that somewhere along the way, he could again try and persuade the captain to hire him to work on the ship. Luck was with him, and White was hired just as he was packing to leave the steamer in Skagway.

He started out serving food to the passengers, and a short while later, he was shifted to mess-man. The messman carried large steaming pots of stew down a ladder into the depths of the ship to the firemen's table, or "mess." All the firemen on board ate together and were responsible for keeping the steam engine fueled with coal. This meant that they had their meals separately from the rest of the ship's crew so they could keep an eye on the engine.

White was thrilled; the farther down into the boat he went, the happier he was. On the way back to Seattle, the steamer got caught in a storm and most people on board were terribly seasick. Funnily enough, this was the most exhilarating part of the trip for White. He did not get sick and, in fact, had never felt better in his life. This was especially unusual because White spent much of his life convinced that he was sick or about to be sick.

Ill Health (Physical and Mental)

White was what might be called a hypochondriac, meaning he had many imaginary illnesses. And it is true that he sometimes thought the worst was happening when he was just a little bit sick. For example, during his first year of college, he was sick for a week and was convinced he had consumption (a kind of tuberculosis). Another time, when he got the stomach flu, he convinced himself he had colon cancer. He did, however, have some real illnesses, too. For example, he suffered from a paratyphoid infection in 1930, and he had lifelong problems with severe hay fever. However, many of his friends didn't take his health complaints seriously. One colleague at the *New Yorker* described him as one of the "strongest and most productive unhealthy [people]"[4] he knew.

But the main thing White suffered from was what is now referred to as depression. White described his symptoms in an essay titled "The Second Tree from the Corner," which was published in the *New Yorker* in 1935. The main character in the story visits the doctor countless times, complaining of symptoms that don't point to any specific illness. These symptoms included dizziness, tight pain at the back of the neck, tightness of the scalp, inability to concentrate, anger at not being able to work, anxiety over work not done, and gas pains. The doctor in the essay responds, "There's nothing wrong with you—you're just scared."[5] Depression was a condition that would come and go throughout White's life.

3 A Lucky Guy

White often liked to say that he was born lucky. This is because the numbers seven (the month of his birth, July) and eleven (the day of his birth) are both lucky in Western popular culture. And White *was* lucky. He was lucky to be born to a well-off, educated family, he was lucky to achieve success early in his writing career, and he was even luckier to become involved with the *New Yorker* magazine as it was starting out.

The *New Yorker*

Returning to New York from his West Coast adventures, White moved back into his parents' home in Mt. Vernon and continued to write poems and other short articles. On February 19, 1925, White bought the first issue of the *New Yorker* from a newsstand in Grand Central Station, a beautiful old train station in New York City. The weekly magazine, which is still published today and continues to be very popular, featured short, humorous articles, light verse, profiles of famous New Yorkers, and reviews of theater, music, art, books, and movies. The magazine also had drawings and one-panel cartoons. It was, and still is, aimed at people who tend to be sophisticated.

White liked the magazine because, as he once described them, its articles were "short, relaxed and sometimes funny."[1] Since this is how White liked to write, it was a perfect match. He soon began submitting pieces to the magazine's editor. The first essay to be accepted and published in May 1925 was a humorous piece titled "In Defense of the Bronx River." People usually made fun of the Bronx River because it was ugly, full of pollution, and often smelled bad. It also flowed by many factories, so it was not what most people would call scenic. In his essay, White jokingly compared it to the Amazon (South America), Danube (Europe), and Mississippi (North America) rivers in its majesty.

Soon, the publisher, Harold Ross, and one of the editors, Katharine S. Angell, realized that they would like to hire White. According to John Updike, a popular adult author and frequent *New Yorker* contributor, Harold Ross (publisher of the *New Yorker*) realized as early as 1926 that White had just the writing style his magazine needed.

Ross and Angell offered White a job several times. Each time he turned them down, shying away from any kind of commitment that involved regular office hours and regimentation. Finally, in 1927, Ross, Angell, and White reached an agreement where White would work half-time for the magazine and they would pay him $30 a week. At the same time, White also worked half-time for an advertising agency. They also paid him $30 a week.

By this point, White had moved to New York City and was sharing a small apartment with three friends. The total rent was $110 a month, so White's portion came to only $27.50 each month. White had plenty of money to spend, and with some of that money, he bought himself his first sailboat.

Gradually, White did more and more work for the magazine. Eventually, he shifted to full-time work at the *New Yorker* and he dropped the advertising agency job. Ross understood that even as a full-time employee, White would not be at his desk during regular office hours. White worked hard, but he was unwilling and unable to keep to any strict schedule. This meant that even though other *New Yorker* employees were in the office from 10 AM to 6 PM, no one ever knew when White would show up. However, Ross knew he could count on White because he never missed a deadline.

This relationship with the *New Yorker* lasted for White's entire writing career. White's contributions to the magazine gave the *New Yorker* its unique voice and, at the same time, the *New Yorker* made White a celebrity. John Updike, a friend and colleague of White's at the magazine, described White as "an incomparably graceful and pungent [penetrating] essayist, and the mainstay [most important part] of [the *New Yorker*] magazine."[2]

Much of White's writing for the magazine appeared in the section called "Notes and Comments." This was a collection of short paragraphs commenting on and observing daily life in New York. Because of the format and the content, "Notes and Comments" was similar to the column White had written for the *Seattle Times*. "Notes and Comments" was written anonymously, meaning that White did not sign those pieces. Nonetheless, readers began to recognize White's "pure yet grave, light yet piercing voice sounding above all other gathered weekly voices."[3]

Lucky in Love

Ultimately, the *New Yorker* would have an even bigger role in White's life than launching his writing career. Through his work at the magazine, White met and fell in love with Katharine Angell, the *New Yorker* editor. They were married on November 13, 1929. White and Katharine wed on the spur of the moment at a Presbyterian church in Bedford Village, New York. Later, White would joke about this momentous event, saying, "I soon realized I had made no mistake in my choice of a wife. I was helping her pack an overnight bag one afternoon when she said, 'Put in some tooth twine.' I knew then that a girl who called dental floss tooth twine was the girl for me. It had been a long search, but it was worth it."[4]

The wedding was so sudden that no one knew about it. White, who, of course, hated public ceremonies and avoided them all his life, commented, "It was a very nice wedding—nobody threw anything, and there was a dog fight."[5]

Understandably, Katharine's children from her first marriage, Roger and Nancy (who were nine and thirteen at the time), had a hard time adjusting to this sudden event. Even the newlyweds themselves were a little nervous about what they had done.

An Unconventional Marriage

In many ways, the Whites' marriage was unconventional. Katharine was a divorcée. Her ex-husband (Ernest Angell) had custody of the children, though Katharine saw them on weekends. Although this is now common, at the time, it was unconventional to get divorced and even more unusual for the father to have the main custody of the children.

Katharine was also seven years older than White and she worked full-time at an important and influential position. In the 1920s and 1930s, it was rare for a middle-class, college-educated woman (she graduated from Bryn Mawr College in Pennsylvania) to work. For the nearly fifty years that Katharine was associated with the *New Yorker*, she was a major force behind it.

Although Katharine's title was fiction editor, she was involved in every major decision at the magazine. For example, when the *New Yorker* was still in its youth, it was Katharine who suggested to the publisher, Harold Ross, that they run serious poetry in addition to the light verse they already published. As fiction editor, she nurtured the writers and artists affiliated with the magazine as if they were her children.

Lifelong Love

Early in their marriage, Katharine wrote to a friend, saying, "If this marriage lasts a year, it'll be worth it."[6] However, the Whites' love was deep and grew more so over the years. And eventually, Roger and Nancy developed a good relationship with White, who was relaxed and patient with them. Also, the Whites had a son, Joel, who was born in 1930.

The Whites were devoted to one another until the day Katharine died of heart failure in 1977. White spent much of his later years helping make sure everyone knew what an important role his wife had played at the *New Yorker* and, by extension, the literary world. He did this by helping one writer work on Katharine's biography and by making sure the gardening columns she had written for the *New Yorker* were published as a collection. The book, *Onward and Upward in the Garden* (1979), included a foreword by White.

Maine

By 1929, White had been living in New York City for four years. In many ways, he loved the city, but he also longed for the country. Ever since his boyhood, he yearned to return to Maine. In 1935, while vacationing in Maine with Katharine, Nancy, Roger, and Joel, White found a twelve-room farmhouse by the sea in North Brooklin, Maine. The property came with thirty-six acres (fifteen hectares).

He and Katharine bought it. At the time, the Whites were still working full-time for the *New Yorker* and living in Manhattan, but they vacationed at their farm every chance they got. Also in 1935, White's father died, and in 1936, his mother died. No matter how old a person is, it is a terrible thing when one's parents die, and White, who was in his mid-thirties, was extremely sad.

Around that same time, White bought a sailboat, a thirty-foot (nine-meter) cutter named

Astrid, which he kept in Maine. A cutter is popular in off-shore sailing because it is easy to reduce the size of the sails. This makes the boat more stable and easier to handle in windy conditions. Sailing embodies much of what White loved. It is a peaceful, contemplative activity that harnesses nature's own power source. It is no accident that White often used the word "shipshape" to describe things. He liked the tidiness that goes along with sailing (everything in its place); he liked the feel of the wind on his face and the calmness he felt while on the water. Sailing for White was a solitary pastime.

As he once said, "I liked to sail alone. The sea was the same as a girl to me—I did not want anyone else along."[7]

4 *Stuart Little*

I n 1938, White persuaded his wife to live full-time in Maine. He also figured out a way to escape the weekly deadlines at the *New Yorker*. White liked writing, but he didn't like feeling rushed, so he arranged to write monthly essays for *Harper's* magazine instead. For four and a half years (1938–1943), he wrote monthly essays that were published in the magazine under the heading "One Man's Meat."

These essays included incidents from his daily life on his farm. He also wrote about the approaching war (World War II), its outbreak, and what part the United States should play in it. Those essays touched on the importance of free speech and other essential freedoms, which showed the continuing influence of Burr, White's Cornell professor. Meanwhile, White still did some work for the *New Yorker*, but not nearly as much as before.

Life in Maine

When they moved to Maine, Katharine resigned as editor of the *New Yorker*, but she became the reviewer of children's literature for the magazine. Katharine could do the reviewing from Maine, although it was complicated. This was well before computers, e-mail, or the Internet, so she couldn't receive or send materials electronically. Every book she was going to review and all of her mail had to be sent to her in Maine. This would take several days. Then she had to mail her reviews (which she typed on a manual type-writer) to the magazine. She then donated all the books she reviewed to the local public library.

The Whites' son, Joel, was about seven when the family permanently moved to North Brooklin. Joel liked living in the big house with the picket fence. A colorful bed of flowers, including holly-hocks, delphiniums, and sweet peas, grew along both sides of the walk. He was pleased to go to a small, rural school two miles (three kilometers) from the farm. Nancy and Roger, Katharine's children from her first marriage, were young adults and away at college. However, they visited the farm during holidays.

In a Dream

For many years, White had been working on a story about a mouse. The idea came to him in 1926, in a dream he was having while sleeping in the upper berth of a train. The train was taking him back home to New York after a visit to Virginia's Shenandoah Valley. As he would later recall, the mouse appeared to him

> nicely dressed, courageous, and questing [seeking or exploring]. When [he] woke up, being a journalist and thankful for small favors, [he] made a few notes about this mouse-child, the only fictional figure ever to have honored and disturbed [his] sleep.[1]

Of course, mice were already kind of a theme in White's life. The first writing prize he had ever won was for a poem about a mouse. Also, once when he had been a young boy and was sick in bed, White had befriended a mouse. In letters he wrote to friends, he claimed to have even tamed the mouse to perform tricks.

A Modest Beginning

Nineteen years after White had the mouse dream, his first children's book, *Stuart Little*, was published. That's a long time between getting an idea and finishing a book. One reason it took a long time for White to write *Stuart Little* is that, originally, he only jotted down short chapters about Stuart in order to tell stories to his eighteen young nieces and nephews. Gradually, however, the manuscript began to take the shape of a book. In 1935, at his wife's urging, White showed the chapters to several publishers whom she knew. However, no one was interested in publishing them.

Then, in 1938, White wrote an essay in "One Man's Meat" (his collection of essays from *Harper's*) about children's literature. Of course, at that time, children's books were overflowing in the Maine house because Katharine was reviewing them. White concluded the essay, saying, "It must be a lot of fun to write for children—reasonably easy work, perhaps even important work."[2] After White's essay appeared in print, several book editors wondered if White was interested in writing for children. By this point in his career,

White had published several books for adults, including collections of poems. However, he'd never written for children.

Once again, he showed a few editors his partially completed manuscript about Stuart the boy mouse. Harper & Brother's Publishing in New York City agreed to publish *Stuart Little* as soon as White finished the last few chapters. However, this would end up taking another six or seven years. Part of what slowed White down was his depression. He described the feeling of being depressed as mice scrambling around in his brain, or having a kite caught in branches. White was also worried about his health because he suffered from things such as unexplained dizzy spells. Because of all of this, he often felt distracted, and it was hard for him to completely focus on writing a book.

His First Children's Book Is Finished

The Whites lived full-time in North Brooklin, Maine, from 1938 to 1944. In 1944, they moved back to New York City to help out at the *New Yorker*. Many regular writers were serving in World War II, and the magazine was desperate for help. Up until this point, White had been struggling to finish *Stuart Little*. The minute he and his wife got settled into an apartment in the Greenwich Village neighborhood of Manhattan, White was inspired to finish the manuscript. He attributed this burst of energy to both the change of scene and a sudden, over-whelming fear that he was about to die. As White later told a friend, "I was almost sure I was about to die, my head felt so queer [strange]."[3] White wanted to put his affairs in order, and he decided he had better finish his book. He finished it just eight weeks after he and his wife returned to New York. (Of course, he also lived another forty years.)

Stuart Little is the second son of the Little family. Although the family is startled when he is born, they are quick to adjust to his being mouse-sized. Mrs. Little puts away the baby clothes she had prepared and sews some doll-sized clothes for Stuart. Mr. Little rigs up a small bed and a way for Stuart to turn on the water faucet by himself. Stuart overcomes all hurdles that come up due to his small size. He is adventurous, courageous, and resourceful.

From the beginning of the book, Stuart, despite being small, is independent. He does chores, like sliding into the drain to retrieve his mother's lost ring and rescuing lost ping-pong balls from under the radiators. His adventures include sailing on a pond in Central Park, driving a miniature, motorized car, and accidentally ending up on a garbage boat in the East River.

Eventually, Stuart meets a small sparrow named Margalo. She comes to stay with the Littles after Mrs. Little finds her injured on the sidewalk. Margalo and Stuart become good friends. Later, when Margalo flies away without saying good-bye, Stuart sets out to find her.

A Big Success

The story was well received by both critics and readers. The book sold 100,000 copies in the first year. To date, almost 4 million copies have been sold, and it has been translated into almost twenty languages. *Stuart Little* was filmed for television by NBC in 1966. In 1999, the book was made into an animated movie, and in 2002, a sequel, *Stuart Little 2*, was released. A sound recording was made of *Stuart Little* in 1973.

As critics John Gillespie and Diana Lembo wrote of *Stuart Little*, "White has created a lively and, [at] times, tender book that is a delight to both the imagination and the emotions."[4] In a 1988 article in the *Horn Book Magazine*, Peter Neumeyer wrote, "I believe that *Stuart Little* is the most inspired, the most surprising, the freshest, the funniest of White's books."[5] Nonetheless, some reviewers complained that readers don't know if Stuart was successful or not in finding Margalo. White's response to such criticism was that the book was meant to be realistic, hence, the plot would not be tied up with a tidy bow. Ultimately, White felt that the story ended in an optimistic way.

Ironically, one influential person who had encouraged White to write a children's book in the first place ended up being strongly critical of his effort. Anne Carroll Moore, who was the first librarian of the children's department at the New York Public Library, was a very strong force in children's literature. When she read a proof of *Stuart Little*, Moore hated it. In fact, after reading the rough draft, Moore wrote a fourteen-page letter to Katharine Angell White explaining why she should urge her husband to withdraw it from publication.

Moore said the book would hurt White's career and that no one would like it. She also wrote a strongly worded letter to White's highly respected and influential publisher, Ursula Nordstrom, who was working at Harper & Brothers. To Nordstrom, Moore voiced two main complaints. One was that it was unnatural for a mouselike creature to be born to a human family. Her other complaint was that the story ends in the beginning or middle of Stuart's quest and doesn't neatly tie up all the loose ends.

However, White felt confident that he had written a good story, though Moore's opposition did get his attention. He responded, saying:

> It is unnerving [nerve-racking] to be told you're bad for children; but I detected in Miss Moore's letter an assumption that there are rules governing the writing of children's literature—rules as inflexible as the rules for lawn tennis. And this I was not sure of. I had followed my instincts in writing about Stuart, and following one's instincts seemed to be the way a writer should operate. I was shook up by the letter but not deflected [disheartened].[6]

White and Stuart

There are several parallels between Stuart and White. For example, both characters are small, but both are tough and resourceful. In some photos, White looks a little mouselike because of his narrow face. Both are perfectionists and like everything neat and tidy and in its place—or ship-shape, as White has referred to in his writing.

White always kept his room neat, even when he was growing up. Stuart's quest for Margalo is a lot like White's trip across the country with Cushman in 1922. In both cases, the characters involved head out for the open road, not pre-cisely sure where they were going, but confident they are heading in the right direction. In the course of the book, Stuart sails on a pond in Central Park, which reflects White's passion for sailing. When White writes of Stuart that he enjoyed having the sea breeze in his face and listening to the sound of the gulls above him, he could just as easily have been describing himself and what he loved about sailing.

5 *Charlotte's Web*

By 1947, the Whites were again living full-time in Maine. There, White would write his next two children's books. White wrote most of the first draft of his most famous book, *Charlotte's Web*, in the spring and summer of 1950. He worked in a boathouse on the shore of his property. The boathouse was very simple. Measuring just 10 feet by 15 feet (3 by 4.5 m), it had a window opening onto the bay and was furnished with a desk, a chair, a bench, a nail keg (a wooden bucket) for a wastebasket, and a wood stove. This, White said, was where he felt most free to write, because there were no distractions.

True Friendship

Charlotte's Web is about a pig named Wilbur who finds out that, eventually, Farmer Zuckerman will turn him into bacon and ham. Wilbur makes friends with a spider named Charlotte, who eventually sets out to save his life. Charlotte does this by weaving words into her web that describe Wilbur: "Some Pig," "Terrific," "Radiant," and "Humble." His owners, the Zuckermans, believe that Wilbur is everything those words say he is, and they decide to enter him in the county fair competition for the best pig. Wilbur wins a special prize, which includes a large medal. After this, his owners vow never to kill him because he is such a special pig.

White often said that the story was a paean to (a hymn to, or appreciation of) life in the barn. Critics loved the book. In a review in the *New York Times Book Review*, novelist Eudora Welty wrote:

> What the book is about is friendship on earth, affection and protection, adventure and miracle, life and death, trust and treachery [deceit], pleasure and pain, and the passing of time. As a piece of work it is just about perfect, and just about magical in the way it is done.[1]

Life on the Farm

People often wonder where White got the idea for *Charlotte's Web*. Since he lived on a farm and loved animals, it is not surprising that animals and farm life would find their way into his books. However, it was a specific incident that took place in his barn that got him thinking about a pig's life. In 1948, White wrote an essay called "Death of a Pig," which was published in *Atlantic Monthly* magazine. In it, White spoke of having a sick pig and how that had upset the balance of life in the barn. White also wrote of the absurdity of nursing a sick pig back to health so that it can then be butchered.

This experience and the subsequent essay started White thinking about how one would go about saving a pig's life. Then, one day, he noticed a large gray spider spinning her web in a corner of his barn, and he started to follow her progress closely. Later, he noticed her making an egg sac, a net of webbing material for holding her eggs. He cut the egg sac from the web, put the sac and the spider in a cardboard box and took it with him to New York City. There, he put the box in his sock drawer and he forgot all about it until a few weeks later, when baby spiders started crawling all over his dresser. White remembered this incident when he began to write the final chapter of the novel that would become *Charlotte's Web*.

At some point, White put the two real-life incidents together and decided to make the pig and the spider friends. He did a lot of research about spiders and was proud of the scientific accuracy in *Charlotte's Web*. For example, his descriptions about Charlotte's cousin, who caught and ate a fish in her web, and of Charlotte's egg sac, her subsequent death, and the post-birth flight of her children are all based on scientific information about spiders.

Fern

Although White wrote the first draft of *Charlotte's Web* fairly quickly, he had a hard time figuring out how to begin the story. He wasn't sure whether to start with Charlotte, or at the barn, or with Wilbur the pig. Finally, he came up with the idea of introducing a little girl named Fern at the very beginning of the story. Although Fern leaves the barn behind her as she grows up and thus fades from the center of the story, her role in the beginning is powerful and dramatic.

In the very first scene of the book, Fern is up early and helping her mother in the kitchen when she sees her father heading to the barn with an ax. When she finds out from her mother that her father is going to kill a baby pig that is the runt of the litter, Fern rushes from the house and confronts her father in the barnyard. "The pig couldn't help being born small, could it," Fern yells at her father. "If I had been very small at birth, would you have killed me?"[2] Fern's father relents and lets Fern have the little pig. Thus, Fern saves Wilbur's life.

By creating the character of Fern, White has woven another layer in the story—the cycle of children growing up and leaving childhood behind. In the course of the book, readers see Fern grow up and lose interest in the barnyard. In this way, the story is about the cycle of seasons in the barn and the cycle of children growing up and losing interest in their childhood pleasures.

Garth Williams, the illustrator for *Stuart Little*, also drew the pictures for *Charlotte's Web*. White's biggest concern was that Williams make Charlotte as lifelike as possible. He sent his publisher a basic book on spiders that had drawings based on observations of actual spiders. He thought the book would help Williams with the drawings. In the end, White was pleased with the illustrations.

Critical Reception

Almost every reviewer recognized that *Charlotte's Web* was outstanding. The year it came out, it became a Newbery Honor book. A review in the *Bulletin of the Center for Children's Books* stated that the book is "an engrossing [absorbing] and amusing story that will appeal to young readers for its realism and humor . . . and that also has a more sophisticated humor and meaning that will appeal to adults."[3] A reviewer in the *Atlantic Monthly* wrote, "If there is such a thing as a realistic fantasy, here it is, and though I am not usually attracted by stories that personify [give a personal nature to] animals, this one is absolutely delicious."[4]

At the same time, many adults tried to read a deeper meaning into the book. In response to this, White would always say that the book was simply what it appeared to be on the surface—a hymn of appreciation to life in the barnyard. As White wrote to an acquaintance, "*Charlotte's Web* is a tale of the animals in my barn, not of the people in my life. When you read it, just relax. Any attempt to find allegorical meanings is bound to end disastrously, for no meanings are in there. I ought to know."[5]

Writing About Death

White was one of the first children's authors to write about death. The critic Gerald Weales observed that *Charlotte's Web* "holds to the idea of death as a fact of life . . . new goslings, another spring. The book is not about the charmed life of Wilbur, but about real life and all that implies."[6] Children's literature critic Sheila Egoff wrote, "*Charlotte's Web* makes death acceptable by dealing with it in terms of the life-and-death cycle of an insect."[7] Another children's literature critic, Peter Neumeyer, called White "one of the pioneers of a growing honesty in children's books."[8]

But White's work is also part of a gradual shift in attitudes toward writing for children. In the nineteenth century, books for young readers were intended to teach a lesson or a moral, but beginning in the twentieth century, writers realized that children's literature could be read for pleasure. Many more authors began writing fantasy, which can engage one's imagination and still convey great truths about things like loyalty, courage, and death. White's books are in a group of classic works such as J. R. R. Tolkien's *The Hobbit* (1938), Kenneth Grahame's *The Wind in the Willows* (1908), and C. S. Lewis's *The Lion, The Witch and the Wardrobe* (1950).

By 1970, about the time that White's last children's book, *The Trumpet of the Swan*, was published, a new type of children's literature was beginning to develop. Authors were confronting real-life issues in a much more explicit way. Writers such as Judy Blume wrote about things young people worried about, including puberty, romantic love, racism, and divorce. Still, at the time that White wrote *Charlotte's Web*, some critics worried that his books raised issues that were not appropriate topics for children's books.

In White's case, though he did not set out to write a book specifically about death, many readers were shocked that Charlotte—a much-loved main character—dies. However, White was writing about life as he saw it. His goal was to write a story to please himself, and in the process of doing so, he has thrilled millions of readers. *Charlotte's Web* has sold more than 20 million copies and has been translated into almost twenty languages, including Welsh, Polish, and three languages spoken in India: Bengali, Marathi, and Telugu.

Top of the Heap

Charlotte's Web stands out today as a phenomenally popular book. For ten years, between 1963 and 1973, *Charlotte's Web* was always on the top ten of the *New York Times* best-seller lists (which are compiled based on bookstore sales). Between 1967 and 1972, it was always first or second. In 1971, it was second only to White's later book, *The Trumpet of the Swan* (1970).

6 *The Trumpet of the Swan*

Beginning in 1961, when she fully retired, Katharine's health began to rapidly decline. Shortly after retiring, she began to get headaches that were so severe, she had to be hospitalized for neurological tests. However, no cause for the pain was found. Later, she had an appendectomy and then a blocked artery, which also required surgery. In 1964, she contracted a dermatitis (a skin disease) that covered her entire body. It was so severe that she couldn't bear the feeling of clothing against her skin. Unfortunately, the medicine she took to relieve her symptoms gave her osteoporosis. Because of this, parts of her spine began to crumble, causing her great pain. These problems were serious enough that, beginning in 1969, Katharine needed around-the-clock nursing care, which was very expensive. Spurred on by Katharine's illnesses as well as his financial concerns, White set out to finish his third children's book. That book, *The Trumpet of the Swan*, was published in 1970 by Harper and Row.

Louis the Swan

The Trumpet of the Swan is about a trumpeter swan, Louis, who is born without a voice. Sam Beaver, a young boy, visits the remote pond where Louis and his family live. Eventually, Sam befriends the swan family. When Louis realizes he can't make any sound, he gets Sam to help him go to school to read and write. Soon, however, Louis realizes that this skill has not solved his problem, since he is the only swan in his flock who can read and write. Meanwhile, he falls in love with a swan named Serena. This, of course, makes him more desperate than ever to find a voice. Sadly, and regardless of his hard work and efforts, Serena doesn't pay attention to him because he cannot make the signature trumpet sound that the other swans do.

In order to help Louis communicate with the other swans, Louis's father decides to steal a trumpet from the nearest music store. Though he feels terrible about doing this, he decides that it is important to help Louis any way he can. Afterward, Louis has a series of adventures, some with Sam and some on his own. Each adventure has the same goal—to earn enough money to repay the music store for the stolen trumpet.

Critical Reception of *Trumpet*

When *The Trumpet of the Swan* first came out, it even outsold *Charlotte's Web*, which was still on the top of the best-seller list for children's books. Critic Zena Sutherland wrote that the story was "a rare delight . . . told with the distinctive blend of calm acceptance and the patently [obviously] ridiculous that have made the author's *Stuart Little* and *Charlotte's Web* classics in their own time."[1] However, some reviewers didn't like it as much as *Charlotte's Web*. They felt that Louis's adventures were too unbelievable and that Sam and Louis's stories weren't woven together as seamlessly as they could have been.

Even White himself was not completely satisfied with the story. He would normally have put it away and let it sit a year before revising and submitting it, but because of the cost of nursing care for Katharine, he felt pressure to earn money. Hence, he submitted it as it was.

Because he felt so rushed, White was not able to wait for Garth Williams, the illustrator of his other two books, to be available for the assignment (at the time, Williams was working in Mexico and wouldn't be home for a few more months). In the end, a different illustrator, Edward Frascino, drew the pictures for *The Trumpet of the Swan*. Both White and Williams were very disappointed when this happened. However, ultimately, White was pleased with Frascino's drawings despite the fact that he would have liked to have collaborated once again with Williams. White always felt that Williams's drawings really brought his books to life.

Difficult Topics

Like White's other books for young readers, *The Trumpet of the Swan* reflects White's love of nature and animals. Like his other books, it also introduces some subjects that were not usually addressed in children's books. For example, Louis's father steals a trumpet. White asks the readers, is it wrong to steal when you desperately want to help your son and feel that you have no other option? This is a complex moral struggle young readers don't usually come across. Louis's father ponders his struggle on his way home from the music store.

> "I have become a thief. What a miserable fate for a bird of my excellent character and high ideas. What led me to commit this awful crime? . . . Why, oh, why did I do this?" Then the answer came to him, as he flew steadily on through the evening sky. "I did it to help my son. I did it for the love of my son Louis."[2]

Some reviewers were nervous that Louis was aware of and shared in his father's moral struggles. They thought this would alarm young readers. Many critics also found the scene where Louis had Sam cut the webs between his toes (so he could play different notes on his trumpet) too violent for children.

White also depicts the complex relationship between Sam and his father very clearly. Although they love each other, Sam keeps some secrets from his dad as he struggles to grow up and become independent. Early in the book, for example, White writes that Sam "felt relieved that he had not told his father about seeing the swans, but he felt queer about it, too. Sam was not a sly boy, but he was odd in one respect: he liked to keep things to himself.

And he liked being alone, particularly when he was in the woods."[3] Several reviewers said the most powerful part of the book was the way in which White showed the relationship between Sam and his father.

What Makes a Good Book

The Trumpet of the Swan was nominated for the National Book Award, but it did not win. However, a book titled *The Summer of the Swans*, by Betsy Byars, did receive the Newbery Medal that year. "How's that for a near miss?" White joked. "I only got one word wrong!"[4] This quip illustrates White's wry sense of humor and his attitude that it wasn't the awards that mattered. Ultimately, for White, it was the writing itself that was more important and meaningful.

A classic book is one that withstands the test of time and continues to be enjoyed by readers of all ages for many decades. Although *The Trumpet of the Swan* is not generally considered the best of White's children's books, it has sold almost 3 million copies to date. It is interesting to notice that not one of White's three children's books won a prestigious award like the Newbery

Medal. However, White accomplished something even better—he wrote three great books that bring pleasure to readers generation after generation. Not many writers can boast of that kind of success.

7 Some Writer

Having suffered very poor health for almost ten years, Katharine died of heart failure in 1977 at the age of eighty-four. White was terribly lonely. Sometimes he would go into town and spend the night at the local small hotel just to have people around him. Then he would return home in the morning. At other times, he would even check himself into the local hospital for a couple of days if he wasn't feeling 100 percent. Because White's son, Joel, and his family lived nearby in North Brooklin, they often visited.

Staying Busy

After such a devastating loss, White tried very hard to remain occupied. Shortly after

Katharine died, a young woman named Linda H. Davis approached White about writing a biography of Katharine. He was happy to help with the project, and he spent many hours answering her questions. He felt strongly that Katharine hadn't received enough recognition and credit for her work as an editor. Davis, who published Katharine's biography in 1987, deeply appreciated working with White. She became a close friend and big fan of his.

In 1985, when he was eighty-six, White died at his home in Maine. His little white farmhouse continued to attract visitors who had become fans of Stuart, Charlotte, and Louis. White had specifically directed that his home remain in private hands, rather than become a museum dedicated to him. After White died, a couple from South Carolina bought the farmhouse. The chicken coop became an artist's studio, and the woodshed became a screened-in porch.

In Love with Writing

When E. B. White received the National Medal for Literature in 1971, he remarked, "I fell in love with the sound of an early typewriter and have been stuck with it ever since. I believed then, as I do now, in the goodness of the published word; it seemed to contain an essential goodness, like the smell of leaf mold."[1] (Leaf mold, a thick layer of decayed leaves that covers the floor of the forest, makes the forest floor feel spongy beneath one's feet. It is full of nutrients that help trees and other plants thrive.) It's hard to imagine someone comparing writing to the smell of leaf mold, but once again, that sort of comparison reflects White's deep connection to the outdoors.

Although he believed in the power and virtue of words, writing wasn't easy for White. When he was working in his study, the long stretches of silence were punctuated by occasional, hesitant bursts of his typewriter. Though White was rarely satisfied with what he wrote, he kept plugging away. He was not a quick writer, but he was steadfast and careful. In letters to friends and colleagues, White often complained about the fact that he wasn't very productive. "I was a writing fool [meaning he wrote constantly] when I was eleven years old and have been tapering off [slowing down] ever since,"[2] he wrote to an admirer. However, this was not really the case. In addition to his three wonderful children's books, White wrote 450 signed pieces and 1,350 unsigned but identifiable columns for the *New Yorker*. Most of these columns were in "Notes and Comments," which, by magazine policy, were unsigned. This comes out to thirty-six pieces a year, or three per month for his almost fifty-year career at the *New Yorker*. This does not include the numerous essays he wrote for other publications.

In Love with Living

Unlike most writers who constantly read what their colleagues are writing and like to talk about writing and literature, White claimed to own only one book that he had read: Henry David Thoreau's *Walden Pond* (1854). This book is about one man's journey into nature and his thoughts on how to live a simple life in harmony with nature. This is also what White thought was important. Although his claim to have only read one book was an exaggeration, White was making the point that he didn't spend much time reading. He spent more time living. And for White, a large part of living meant sailing and tending to his animals.

On days when the weather was good for sailing, he would drive down to the North Brooklin public dock in his dark blue Mercedes sedan, row out to his sailboat, rig it (put the sails up and get ready to go), and head off for the open ocean. In 1969, he wrote to a friend:

> Writing . . . is hard work for me and usually not attended with any joy. It has its satisfactions, but the act of writing is often a pure headache, and I don't kid myself about there being any joy in it. When I want some fun, I don't write, I go sailing.[3]

Throughout his life, White would own four sailboats. The first was a boat named *Pequod*, which he bought in his twenties, the second was the *Astrid*, which he bought in 1925. His next boat he named *Fern*, and the fourth and final boat he named *Martha*, after his son Joel's daughter. Joel inherited White's love of sailing and the sea. In fact, Joel grew up to be a master boat builder, and he actually built White's fourth and last boat, *Martha*.

White's other lifelong pleasure was tending to his animals. At one point, he had fifteen sheep, 150 chickens, six roosters, three geese, a dog, a tomcat, a pig, and a captive mouse on his farm. Tending to his animals and the daily chores they required kept White humble. "'Humble' has two meanings. It means 'not proud' and it means 'near the ground,'"[4] as Charlotte explains in *Charlotte's Web*. In White's case, "near the ground" meant both connected to the land and the world in a very direct way—through his animals and his farm. It also meant he saw himself as a common man, no wiser or more literary than anyone else.

White wrote from this humble perspective, and his readers loved him for it. In Scott Elledge's biography of White, Elledge wrote that E. B. White spoke to his readers

> in a way that comforted them and encouraged them as well as entertained them . . . what counted was not only what he said but what kind of a man he seemed to be . . . [he] projected the character of a sensitive, thoroughly honest, decent, and reliable human being with a sense of humor that was modest, self-knowing, and good-natured . . . he didn't sound like someone who thought of himself as a writer or literary person. He was simply a busy, thoughtful man who, when writing, was snatching time from something else.[5]

Writing for Children

White had very strong opinions about writing for children. When he received the Laura Ingalls Wilder Award, White wrote:

> I have two or three strong beliefs about the business of writing for children. I feel I must

never kid them about anything. I feel I must be on solid ground myself. I also feel that a writer has an obligation to transmit, as best he can, his love of life, his appreciation for the world. I am not averse to [against] departing from reality, but I am against departing from the truth.[6]

White often worried that he would never make a lasting contribution to the world of letters, since most of his essays were about current affairs. However, that was not to be the case. As Peter Neumeyer wrote, "E. B. White has a firm place in American letters as a distinguished essayist, a man who expressed his wry view of the world in exquisitely chiseled sentences. Applying that same craft to three books for children, E. B. White has won a place in the hearts of the young forever."[7]

Interview with E. B. White

The following interview of E. B. White by Justin Wintle was excerpted from *The Pied Pipers: Interviews with the Influential Creators of Children's Literature*, edited by Justin Wintle and Emma Fisher. The book, published by Paddington Press in 1974, contains interviews with some of the great names in modern children's literature.

JUSTIN WINTLE: Many outstanding American authors have also been journalists. Why is this? And what in your view does journalism do for a writer who has other ambitions?

E. B. WHITE: I was a journalist first, an author second. A good deal of my life was spent with the *New Yorker*—I was a commentator, a reporter, and a memoirist. I submitted every-thing that came into my head and out of my typewriter, including poems. Journalism, the life of quick action and deadlines, is good discipline for a writer, and I still have the instincts and habits of a journalist, though I am no longer actively engaged in writing for a periodical.

JUSTIN WINTLE: All your books, for young and old readers alike, are characterized by elegance and humor. Where did these qualities come from?

E. B. WHITE: If, as you suggest, there is any elegance, any humor in my work, I haven't the slightest idea of the source of such qualities. When humor shows up in a person's writing, it seems to me it is because the writer has a natural awareness of the curious ironies and juxtapositions of life. Jane Austen seldom wrote anything funny, but her novels are masterpieces of humorous expression.

JUSTIN WINTLE: On the subject of humor, does it come out of the fantasy in your children's books? Or does the fantasy come out of the humor? If I am making an impossible distinction, could you please say why?

E. B. WHITE: When you ask whether, in my books for children, the humor comes out of the fantasy, or whether it is the other way around, you are asking me a question I can't answer. I would think that fantastical episodes or situations have a tendency to evoke humor. A lot depends, I suppose, on what a writer does with his material. There is a place in *Charlotte's Web* where the pig boasts that he can spin a web, and he makes a try at it. Perhaps there is something essentially comical about a pig trying to spin a web—I don't know. But whether there is or isn't, the way a writer develops the theme is crucial.

JUSTIN WINTLE: What are the differences between writing for children and writing for adults in your experience?

E. B. WHITE: In my experience, the only difference (save for a very slight modification of vocabulary) is in one's state of mind. Children are a wonderful audience—they are so eager, so receptive, so quick. I have great respect for their powers of observation and reasoning. But like any good writer, I write to amuse myself, not some imaginary audience, and I rather suspect that it is a great help if one has managed never really to grow up. Some writers, I have noticed, have a tendency to write down to children. That way lies disaster. Other writers feel they must use only the easy words, the familiar words. I use any word I feel like using, on the theory that children enjoy new encounters and that I don't gain anything by depriving myself of the full scope of the language. When I mentioned a "very slight modification of vocabulary," I was really alluding to the state of one's mind—which has an effect on the state of one's vocabulary.

JUSTIN WINTLE: In *Stuart Little* the book opens with a woman giving birth to a mouse. There would be something nauseous about this if it happened in an adult novel, but in a children's book it can stand. Does this point to something essential about what a children's book is?

E. B. WHITE: The arrival of Stuart as the second son of Mrs. Frederick C. Little would have been completely unacceptable had I entertained any monstrous ideas about the matter, or had I introduced it gradually and in detail. It all happens in the first sentence and without the slightest suggestion of anything untoward or disagreeable. You have to make the leap boldly, if you are going to jump at all. As the story develops, it becomes clear that Stuart is a boy who happens to look like a mouse. The whole business is so fantastical as to rule out any anatomical embarrassment, such as a woman giving birth to a mouse. The first chapter of *Stuart Little* was written about fifty years ago, and in that innocent day children were not privy to the facts of life. Today, they are better informed about mammalian birth [how mammals are born], and I suppose a few of them have moments of wondering about Stuart. But for the most part they accept the event without question, which is the happy approach.

JUSTIN WINTLE: What made you want to write your three books for children? Were they in fact written for children? And (the obvious question I'm afraid) what were the origins of each one?

E. B. WHITE: My first book for children was not begun with book publication in mind. I had a small son and several small nephews and nieces, and occasionally I wrote an episode in the hope of amusing them. A dozen years or more went by before *Stuart Little* emerged as a book. My second book for children was written because I had an urge to bring the characters in my own barnyard into a sustained story. I used to raise a spring pig, for butchering in the fall, and I never much cared for this deliberate murder, so I invented a way to save a pig's life. *Charlotte's Web* was an easy book for me to write because of my intimate connection with the main characters. I wrote *The Trumpet of the Swan* when I was visited by the idea of a Trumpeter Swan who came into the world without a voice.

JUSTIN WINTLE: There are two themes common to all three of your children's books. The first is the anthropomorphic one, the animal as a participant in human society. How would you compare your kind of anthropomorphism with that of other writers (e.g., Richard Adams in *Watership Down* or Kipling's *Jungle Books* or the *Doctor Doo-Little* books)? Is it a means of gentle satire?

E. B. WHITE: I think all anthropomorphism is satirical. I can't compare my kind with the style of other writers—I'll leave that to somebody else.

JUSTIN WINTLE: The second theme is that each of your characters struggles against and masters incredible odds. Louis the Swan overcomes his muteness by learning the trumpet; Wilbur the pig is saved from slaughter when his friend Charlotte the Spider learns to write inside her web; and Stuart Little simply manages to survive. Is this a theme you have been aware of?

E. B. WHITE: None of my books was written to a theme. Life is a struggle, and there is always the question of survival uppermost. So it is not surprising that these three stories, although completely different one from the other, have a common thread running through them.

JUSTIN WINTLE: Given the similarities of your three children's books, how in your opinion have you developed as a children's writer?

E. B. WHITE: I don't understand your ninth question. There is some question as to my having "developed" as a children's writer. I may just have been going downhill without knowing it.

JUSTIN WINTLE: When *Stuart Little* was still in manuscript it was deplored by Anne Carroll Moore, then a leading authority on children's literature in the States. Many years later you wrote a piece claiming that her response was based on a judgment that you had broken certain "inflexible rules" when writing for children. What were those inflexible rules, and how have they changed since then?

E. B. WHITE: I can't say what was in Anne Carroll Moore's mind when she tried to get me to withdraw the manuscript of *Stuart Little*. I think she was dead set against an American family having a mouse-boy. I think, too, she found my story inconclusive (which it is), and it seems to me she said something about its having been written by a sick mind. I may be misquoting her, as I haven't got the letter in my possession. There were undoubtedly some rules a writer was supposed to follow when writing for children, and I guess I smashed a few of them, knowingly or unknowingly. Today, all rules are off; the sky is the limit.

JUSTIN WINTLE: When you wish to "make a point" in your children's books you do it by humorous demonstration, never by preaching. The term "low seriousness" I expect would make you jump; but what would you call it?

E. B. WHITE: A writer who isn't "serious" isn't a writer at all. My books are serious books. But a man doesn't have to give up jumping and dancing and singing just because he is a serious man. I dive into a story the way I dive into the sea, prepared to splash about and make merry.

JUSTIN WINTLE: Several critics have found that the ending of *Stuart Little* is inconclusive—in fact a non-ending. Do you ever feel the same way about it? Can something which is essentially humorous in fact have an ending?

E. B. WHITE: There have been complaints about the ending of *Stuart Little*. Children, by and large, want to know whether Stuart ever found Margalo, and whether he got home. But I deliberately left the matter hanging. The story is [that] of a quest—specifically, the quest for beauty. Life is essentially inconclusive, in most respects, and a "happy" ending would have been out of key with the story of Stuart's search. Once in a while, to my great delight, a young reader perceives this and writes me a letter of approbation.

JUSTIN WINTLE: Both *Stuart Little* and *The Trumpet of the Swan* contain school scenes, lessons in which conventional methods of teaching are sent up [made fun of]. Is this because you object to the way you were educated?

E. B. WHITE: The schoolroom scenes in *Stuart* and *The Trumpet* got in there naturally. I did not introduce them, or concoct them, in order to comment on my own schooling. I was educated in a period when schoolrooms were dull and unimaginative, when discipline was firm, and when not much effort was made to give scholars free rein. If the schoolrooms in my books are a bit on the disorderly side, perhaps it is a subconscious attempt on my part to raise a rumpus and break the monotony. But I am glad I went to schools that made no bones about teaching me to read and write and spell. Too many youngsters nowadays enter college not knowing how to read and write and spell, more's the pity. Even a monotonous atmosphere has its virtues, for it compels the scholar to invent ways to lift himself out of his boredom, and sometimes this takes the form of creation.

JUSTIN WINTLE: "People believe almost anything they see in print"—the Spider's excuse in *Charlotte's Web*. Is that true? And in what sense would a child "believe" in the fantasies you have created?

E. B. WHITE: Children obviously enjoy fantastical events. The dullards among them soberly question the happenings and ask, "Is it true?" But most children are quite able to absorb and enjoy fantasy without questioning it, even when they are aware that they are momentarily inhabiting a world quite different from the real one.

JUSTIN WINTLE: In *Charlotte's Web* you make it a point that the girl, Fern, never talks to any of the animals, only listens to what they say. Why did you stop there?

E. B. WHITE: In *Charlotte's Web* there is no conversation between animals and people. Animals talk to animals, people talk to people. Fern is a listener, and a translator. This is basic to the story. It also provides a story that is much closer to reality. Animals do converse—not in English words, but they converse.

JUSTIN WINTLE: Perhaps *Charlotte's Web* is your most popular book because its characters are so fully blown. Did they just come from what you considered the nature of the animals in question, or were they derived from elsewhere too? Is Templeton unscrupulous simply because he is a rat, or because he reminds you of someone as well?

E. B. WHITE: The characters in *Charlotte's Web* were based on the animals I happened to be living among—the spider, the rat, the pig, the geese, the sheep. Templeton does not remind me of anyone—he is unscrupulous because he is a rat.

JUSTIN WINTLE: What is the appeal of writing children's books to you?

E. B. WHITE: It amuses me to write children's books—perhaps that is what you mean when you ask, "What is the appeal . . . " But I am not mainly a writer of children's stories. For every children's book I've written, I have written four adult books.

JUSTIN WINTLE: Have there been distinct influences? What was the effect of working with [James] Thurber? Were you brought up on [Mark Twain's] *Huckleberry Finn*?

E. B. WHITE: I was not brought up on *Huckleberry Finn*. And I don't recall that working with Thurber had any profound influence on me, although it was a pleasure.

JUSTIN WINTLE: Have you read the work of other contemporary children's writers? If so, whom would you single out for praise or scorn?

E. B. WHITE: I am not well-read in contemporary literature for children and am not in a good position to comment on other authors.

Timeline

July 11, 1899 Elwyn Brooks White is born in Mt. Vernon, New York.

1917–1921 White attends Cornell University in Ithaca, New York.

1925 White's first article is published in the *New Yorker*.

1929 White marries Katharine S. Angell.

1930 Their son, Joel, is born.

1935 White's father, Samuel, dies.

1936 White's mother, Jessie, dies of cancer.

1938 White moves to Maine from New York City.

1944 White returns to New York City from Maine. He continues to summer in Maine.

1945 *Stuart Little*, White's first book for young readers, is published.

1947 White moves permanently to North Brooklin, Maine.

1948 White receives honorary degrees from Yale, Dartmouth, and the University of Maine.

1952 *Charlotte's Web*, White's second book for young readers, is published.

1954 White receives honorary degrees from Harvard and Colby colleges.

1960 White receives the Gold Medal for *Essays and Criticism* from the National Institute of Arts and Letters.

1961 Katharine White retires from the *New Yorker*.

1963 White is named one of thirty-one to receive the Medal of Freedom from President Kennedy.

1970 *The Trumpet of the Swan*, White's third and final book for young readers, is published. White receives the Laura Ingalls Wilder Award from the children's services division of the American Library Association (ALA).

1971 White receives the National Medal for Literature from the National Book Committee.

1973 White is elected to the American Academy of Arts and Letters. *Charlotte's Web* is made into an animated film with Debbie Reynolds as the voice of Charlotte.

1977 Katharine White dies of congestive heart failure on July 20.

1978 White receives a special Pulitzer Prize citation for his lifetime achievements in arts and letters.

1985 White dies at home in North Brooklin, Maine.

List of
Selected Works

Charlotte's Web. New York: Harper &
    Brothers, 1952.

The Elements of Style (editorial supervisor
    and contributor), by William Strunk Jr.
    New York: Macmillan, 1979.

Stuart Little. New York: Harper &
    Brothers, 1945.

The Trumpet of the Swan. New York:
    Harper & Row, 1970.

List of
Selected Awards

Member, American Academy of Arts and
    Letters (only fifty members in the society)
George G. Stone Center for Children's Books
    Recognition of Merit Award (1970) for
    Charlotte's Web
Honorary Degree, Bowdoin College (1950)
Honorary Degree, Colby College (1954)
Honorary Degree, Dartmouth College (1948)
Honorary Degree, Hamilton College (1952)
Honorary Degree, Harvard University (1954)
Honorary Degree, University of Maine (1948)
Honorary Degree, Yale University (1948)
Laura Ingalls Wilder Award for "lasting con-
    tribution to children's literature" (1970)

National Association of Independent
  Schools Award (1955) for "The Second
  Tree from the Corner"

National Book Award nomination for *The
  Trumpet of the Swan* (1971)

National Institute of Arts and Letters for *Essays
  and Criticism*, Gold Medal (1960)

Newbery Medal runner-up for *Charlotte's Web*

Presidential Medal of Freedom (1963)

Pulitzer Prize, special citation for lifetime
  achievement (1978)

Glossary

absurdity Something that is ridiculous.

advocate Someone who strongly believes in and defends a cause.

allegorical Having a deeper hidden meaning or message.

berth A place on a ship or boat where someone sleeps.

Bryn Mawr A women's college in Bryn Mawr, Pennsylvania.

concession A small stand that sells food or souvenirs.

concise Brief, with no wasted words or thoughts.

contemplative Thoughtful.

coveted Greatly desired.

critiqued Made suggestions and comments.

cutter A type of sailboat with two sails: the jib, a small sail in front, and a mainsail, or staysail.

devastated Very upset.

divorcée A woman who is divorced.

editor in chief The title of the person who is in charge of putting a publication together.

embodies Gives concrete form to an idea or concept.

ethics A code of behavior that follows rules of fairness and justice.

exhilarating Very exciting.

fauna Animals native to a specific area.

flora Plants native to a specific area.

footloose Free to go and do as one pleases. Having no responsibilities.

harnesses Uses.

hay fever An allergy caused by pollen or dust.

hay hand Someone who works harvesting and baling hay.

incubator A heated, protected box that keeps eggs warm enough to hatch.

Irish setter A large-sized dog with long, reddish fur.

ironic Use of words to mean something different, and often opposite, from their literal meaning.

Laura Ingalls Wilder Award An award given every five years by the Children's Services Division of the American Library Association (ALA) to a writer whose books published in the United States "have over a period of years made a substantial and lasting contribution to literature for children."

leaf mold Thick carpet of decaying leaves found on the floor of the woods.

Longfellow, Henry Wadsworth (1807–1882) A popular American poet.

majesty Impressive beauty and dignity.

Manhattan A borough (district) of New York City.

Middle Ages A period of European history that lasted from about 476 to 1453.

Model T The first mass-produced automobile. More than 15 million were made and sold in the United States between 1908 and 1927. The cars ranged in price from $280 to $950.

mongrel An animal (usually a dog) of mixed breeds; mutt.

neurological Having to do with the nervous system.

octagonal Having eight sides.

optimistic Thinking positive thoughts; looking on the bright side of a situation.

osteoporosis A disease characterized by the loss of calcium in bones.

paean A hymn, or way to praise something.

partial Not complete.

Presidential Medal of Freedom Established in 1963, the award recognizes individuals who have made an "especially meritorious contribution to national security or national interests of the United States or to world peace or to cultural or other significant public or private endeavors."

proof The form a book or article is in just before it is published. It gives the author and the publisher an idea of how the book will look when it is printed.

prose The ordinary form of written language, as compared to poetry.

quip A clever saying or remark.

regimentation Rules and schedules.

relents Gives in.

rig Put together. In the case of a sailboat, hoisting sails and generally making ready to sail.

runt Smallest and weakest animal in a litter.

ruts Grooves worn into dirt roads by car tires.

savior Someone who saves someone else.

signature Something, such as a style or logo, that represents a person.

slate A smooth stone, usually dark gray, used in buildings.

steadfast Loyal, dedicated.

touring book A book of driving maps and descriptions of various sights to see. Used by people traveling by car.

vivacious Lively, full of energy.

Welty, Eudora (1909–2001) An American short-story writer and novelist best known for her stories about people and life in the deep South. She won the Pulitzer Prize for her novel *The Optimist's Daughter* (1972).

wry A kind of dry humor, a little bit mocking or sarcastic.

yearned Longed for, desired very much.

For More Information

Due to the changing nature of Internet links, the Rosen Publishing Group, Inc., has developed an online list of Web sites related to the subject of this book. This site is updated regularly. Please use this link to access the list:

http://www.rosenlinks.com/lab/ebwh

For Further Reading

Commire, Anne, ed. *Something About the Author*, volume 29. Detroit, MI: Gale Research, 1982.

Gherman, Beverly. *E. B. White: Some Writer!* New York: Atheneum, 1992.

Neumeyer, Peter F., and Anita Silvey, eds. *Children's Books and Their Creators*. New York: Houghton Mifflin Company, 1995.

Tingum, Janice. *E. B. White: The Elements of a Writer*. Minneapolis, MN: Lerner Publishing Group, 1995.

Bibliography

Agosta, Lucien L. *E. B. White: The Children's Books*. New York: Twayne Publishers, 1995.

Block, Ann, and Carolyn Riley, eds. *Children's Literature Review*, volume 1. Detroit, MI: Gale Research Company, 1976.

Collins, David R. *To the Point: A Story About E. B. White*. Minneapolis, MN: Carolrhoda Books, 1989.

Commire, Anne, ed. *Something About the Author*, volume 2. Detroit, MI: Gale Research, 1971.

Commire, Anne, ed. *Something About the Author*, volume 29. Detroit, MI: Gale Research, 1982.

Davis, Linda H. "The Man on the Swing," *New Yorker*, volume 69, December 27, 1993.

Davis, Linda H. *Onward and Upward: A Biography of Katharine S. White*. New York: Harper & Row Publishers, 1987.

"E. B. White." Books and Writers Web Site. Retrieved January 2004 (http://www.kirjasto.sci.fi/ebwhite.htm).

E. B. White Official Web Site. Retrieved January 2004 (www.ebwhitebooks.com).

Elledge, Scott. *E. B. White: A Biography*. New York: W. W. Norton & Company, 1984.

Fuller, Muriel, ed. *More Junior Authors*. New York: H. W. Wilson, 1963.

Gherman, Beverly. *E. B. White: Some Writer!* New York: Atheneum, 1992.

Gill, Brendan. *Here at the New Yorker*. New York: Random House, 1975.

Hedblad, Alan, ed. *Something About the Author*, volume 100. Detroit, MI: Gale Research, 1999.

McElmeel, Sharron L., ed. *100 Most Popular Children's Authors: Biographical Sketches and Bibliographies*. Englewood, CO: Libraries Unlimited, Inc., 1999.

Neumeyer, Peter F., and Anita Silvey, eds. *Children's Books and Their Creators*. New York: Houghton Mifflin Company, 1995.

Neumeyer, Peter F. "Stuart Little: The Manuscripts," *Horn Book*

Magazine, September/October 1988, pp. 593–600.

New Yorker. "Notes and Comments," October 14, 1985, pp. 31–33.

Root, Robert L., Jr. *Critical Essays on E. B. White*. New York: G. K. Hall & Co., 1994.

Russell, Isabel. *Katharine and E. B. White: An Affectionate Memoir*. New York: W. W. Norton and Company, 1988.

Sampson, Edward C. *E. B. White*. New York: Twayne Publishers, Inc., 1974.

Shenker, Israel. "E. B. White, Notes and Comment by Author," July 11, 1969, *New York Times*. Retrieved January 8, 2004 (http://www.nytimes.com/books/97/08/03/lifetimes/white-notes.html).

Strunk, William, Jr., and E. B. White. *The Elements of Style*, fifth edition. New York: Longman Publishing, 2000.

Tingum, Janice. *E. B. White: The Elements of a Writer*. Minneapolis, MN: Lerner Publishing Group, 1995.

Updike, John. "Magnum Opus," *New Yorker*, July 12, 1999.

Welty, Eudora. "Life in the Barn Was Very Good," *New York Times Book Review*, October 19, 1952.

White, E. B. "A Boy I Knew," *Reader's Digest*, volume 36, no. 218, June 1940, pp. 33–36.

White, E. B. *Charlotte's Web*, fiftieth anniversary retrospective edition with afterword by Peter F. Neumeyer. New York: Harper-Collins Publishers, 2002.

White, E. B. *Essays of E. B. White*. New York: Harper & Row Publishers, 1977.

White, E. B. "Laura Ingalls Wilder Acceptance," *Horn Book Magazine*, August 1970, pp. 349–351.

White, E. B. *Letters of E. B. White*. New York: Harper Colophone Books, 1976.

White, E. B. *Stuart Little*. New York: Harper & Row Publishers, 1945.

White, E. B. *The Trumpet of the Swan*. New York: Harper & Row Publishers, 1970.

Wintle, Justin, and Emily Fisher. *The Pied Pipers: Interviews with the Influential Creators of Children's Literature*. New York: Paddington Press, Ltd., 1974, pp. 126–131.

Source Notes

Introduction

1. Scott Elledge, *E. B. White: A Biography* (New York: W. W. Norton & Company, 1984), p. 300.
2. Edward C. Sampson, *E. B. White* (New York: Twayne Publishers, Inc., 1974), p. 95.
3. Justin Wintle and Emily Fisher, *The Pied Pipers: Interviews with the Influential Creators of Children's Literature* (New York: Paddington Press, Ltd. 1974), p. 127.
4. *The New Yorker*, "Notes and Comments," October 14, 1985, p. 31.

Chapter 1

1. Scott Elledge, *E. B. White: A Biography* (New York: W. W. Norton & Company, 1984), p. 23.
2. E. B.White, *The Trumpet of the Swan* (New York: Harper & Row, 1970), p. 23.

3. E. B. White, *Letters of E. B. White*, collected and edited by Dorothy Lobrano Guth (New York: Harper Colophon Books, 1976), p. 281.

Chapter 2

1. E. B.White, *Essays of E. B. White* (New York: Harper & Row Publishers, 1977), p. 259.
2. Scott Elledge, *E. B. White: A Biography* (New York: W. W. Norton & Company, 1984), p. 59. Text was originally from E. B. White's Memorial Day speech at Cornell University, May 1940.
3. Israel Shenker, "E. B. White, Notes and Comment by Author," July 11, 1969, *New York Times*. Retrieved January 8, 2004 (http://www.nytimes.com/books/97/08/03/lifetimes/white-notes.html).
4. Brendan Gill, *Here at the New Yorker* (New York: Random House, 1975), p. 293.
5. E. B. White, *The Second Tree from the Corner* (New York: Harper & Row Publishers, 1935), p. 97.

Chapter 3

1. E. B. White, *Letters of E. B. White*, collected and edited by Dorothy Lobrano Guth (New York, Harper Colophon Books, 1976), p. 72.
2. John Updike, "Magnum Opus," *New Yorker*, July 12, 1999.
3. Ibid.
4. E. B. White, *Letters of E. B. White*, p. 84.
5. Ibid., p. 83.

6. Linda H. Davis, *Onward and Upward: A Biography of Katharine S. White* (New York: Harper & Row Publishers, 1987), p. 99.
7. E. B. White, *Essays of E. B. White* (New York: Harper & Row Publishers, 1977), pp. 205–207.

Chapter 4

1. Scott Elledge, *E. B. White: A Biography* (New York: W. W. Norton & Company, 1984), p. 253. Text originally appeared in the *New York Times Book Review*, May 24, 1970.
2. Ibid., p. 254.
3. Ibid., p. 254.
4. John Gillespie and Diana Lembo, *Introducing Books: A Guide for the Middle Grades* (New York: R. R. Bowker, 1970), p. 259.
5. Peter F. Neumeyer, "Stuart Little: The Manuscripts," *Horn Book Magazine*, September/October 1988, p. 600.
6. Scott Elledge, p. 263.

Chapter 5

1. Eudora Welty, "Life in the Barn Was Very Good," *New York Times Book Review*, October 19, 1952, p. 49.
2. E. B. White, *Charlotte's Web* (New York: HarperCollins Publishers, 1952), p. 3.
3. *Bulletin of the Center for Children's Books*, published by the University of Chicago. December 1952, p. 36.

4. Lucien Agosta, *E. B. White: The Children's Books* (New York: Twayne Publishers, 1995), p. 117.

5. E. B. White, *Letters of E. B. White,* collected and edited by Dorothy Lobrano Guth (New York: Harper Colophone Books, 1976), p. 373.

6. Gerald Weales, "The Designs of E. B. White," in *Authors and Illustrators of Children's Books,* edited by Mariam Hoffman and Eva Samuels (New York: R. R. Bowker, 1970), pp. 409–410. Text originally appeared in the *New York Times Book Review,* May 24, 1970.

7. Sheila Egoff, G. T. Stubbs, and L. F. Ashley, eds., *Only Connect: Readings on Children's Literature* (Toronto: Oxford University Press, 1969), p. 431.

8. Peter F. Neumeyer, "Afterword," in *Charlotte's Web Fiftieth Anniversary Retrospective Edition* (New York: HarperCollins Publishers, 2002), p. 208.

Chapter 6

1. Zena Sutherland, *The Best in Children's Books* (Chicago: The University of Chicago Press, 1973), p. 422.

2. E. B. White, *The Trumpet of the Swan* (New York: Harper & Row Publishers, 1970), p. 80.

3. Ibid., p. 3.

4. E. B. White, *Letters of E. B. White*, collected and edited by Dorothy Lobrano Guth (New York: Harper Colophone Books, 1976), p. 615.

Chapter 7

1. Anne Commire, ed. *Something About the Author*, volume 29 (Detroit, MI: Gale Research, 1982), page 236.
2. Ibid., p 229.
3. E. B. White, *Letters of E. B. White*, collected and edited by Dorothy Lobrano Guth (New York: Harper Colophone Books, 1976), p. 582.
4. E. B. White, *Charlotte's Web* (New York: Harper-Collins Publishers, 1952), p. 140.
5. Scott Elledge, *E. B. White: A Biography* (New York: W. W. Norton & Company, 1984), pp. 219–220.
6. E. B. White, "Laura Ingalls Wilder Acceptance," *Horn Book Magazine*, August 1970, p. 350.
7. Peter F. Neumeyer, in *Children's Books and Their Creators*, edited by Anita Silvey (New York: Houghton Mifflin Company, 1995), pp. 676–678.

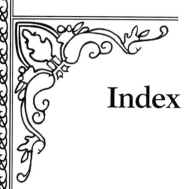

Index

About the Author

This is Deb Aronson's first children's book. She has been an E. B. White fan all her life and still has her copy of *Stuart Little*, inscribed to her by her own grandmother in 1966. Although this is the first time she has written about a writer, she has written articles about many other interesting people, including an archaeologist, a landscape photographer, a male midwife, and a geologist studying the center of the earth. Deb lives in Urbana, Illinois, with her two children, her husband, and her black cat named Sid.

Photo Credits

Cover, p. 2 © Bettmann/Corbis.

Series Designer: Tahara Anderson; **Editor:** Annie Sommers